Intro

Handing students their degrees upon graduation for the first time was a gratifying experience. It was also a humbling one.

As I watched them walk across the stage toward me, a smile on their faces and a proud (and sometimes broke) family in the audience, I couldn't help but ask myself if they were truly ready for what came next.

That feeling led to a series of conversations I now have with our students at Art Center throughout the course of their program, culminating with our grad dinner the night before commencement. Those conversations are the basis of this book.

In it, I've tried to take all of my experiences, from my early years just out of school to my years at the highest levels of business and condense the lessons I've lived and learned into a few short, easily understandable words of advice.

I hope you find them helpful.

This
is your
ticket
to learn.

I heard a story from a friend of mine about a guy who got his private pilot's license in Texas. When the FAA examiner handed it to him, he said, "here, this is your ticket to learn."

That's exactly what your diploma is.

Far from an end to your period of learning, your transition into the working world is just the beginning.

And if you don't view it that way, you will quickly find yourself falling behind.

Yes, you have valuable attributes that should enable you to begin contributing at work on day one. But the best thing that can be said about your "formal" education is that it's a solid base on which to begin building your "real" education.

I learned more and improved more during my first year of work than I did in the three or four previous years combined.

You should too, about your profession, about yourself, about life.

Learn by listening.

Learn by watching.

Learn by asking.

And most of all, learn by doing and doing and doing.

A work
work
work life
balance.

If you're just beginning your career and you're worried about work/life balance, you probably won't be very successful.

Success requires passion.

Passion and balance are incongruous.

The happiest people I know have matched their ambitions with a clear understanding of what's required to achieve them.

They love what they do and view it as an integral part of their life, not a sacrifice that takes them away from their life.

If your priority is to be the best in the world at what you do or start the next Apple, don't expect to be driving home while it's still light outside or going fishing every weekend.

Unless your goal is to be the best in the world at fishing.

Mentors come in different flavors.

When we hear the word "mentor", we tend to think of a kind, patient, wise, nurturing sage-like figure that has our best interests at heart. And in fact, you may be fortunate enough to come across someone who fits this description.

More likely, you will have a collection of influences throughout your career, each for different reasons, and many of whom you won't recognize as mentors until long after the fact.

Some may actually talk to you and teach you.

Some will not even know you exist, but you will learn from by watching.

Some will be role models for the inspiring work they do.

Some will be role models for the way they carry themselves.

Some will be role models for the way they lead people and build teams.

Some will be role models for the way they deal with adversity.

Some will be role models for their persistence and longevity.

And some, will be role models for what NOT to become.

Learn from them all, and commit yourself to becoming a positive mentor for those who follow you.

Small goals are big.

Big goals are easy.

Big goals are fun.

I will be famous. I will be rich. I will become a CEO. I will start a company.
I will sell a company.

But it's the small goals that make the big goals happen.

And small goals are hard.

I will take on two additional assignments every week.

I will put in eight hours every weekend working on an entrepreneurial idea.

I will stay an hour later at work every day working on an "extra credit"
project that will pay nothing but get me noticed within the company.

An analogy I like to use is about someone who aspires to be a better
photographer.

Writing down "I will become a better photographer" will get you nowhere.

Writing down "I will shoot 30 photographs a day for the next twelve
months" (and then actually doing it) will make you a better photographer.

Make your own luck.

I don't deny the existence of luck in business.

But from my experience, 95% of what appears to be luck is actually the result of someone making conscious choices that led to an opportunity that they were then able to take advantage of.

Taking on more assignments and doing them well will obviously increase the odds of one of them becoming your "breakout" moment.

Spending what could have been your free time building work relationships or working on entrepreneurial side projects may not pay dividends for years but could ultimately change the arc of your entire life.

Doing all of the small, over-and-above-the-call-of-duty things every day that most people would consider a waste of time can have a powerful cumulative effect.

And when they lead to a major promotion or the launching of your own business, you'll have the added perk of listening to everyone whisper about how "lucky" you are.

No
one
cares.

When you are not feeling well.

When you have boyfriend/girlfriend issues.

When you have family issues.

When you have money issues.

When your car won't start.

When your internet is down.

When you lose your phone.

When your rent is due.

When you're tired.

When you're bored with your work.

When you need a vacation.

When your dog is sick.

When you have a hangover.

They only care that you do what you've committted to do.

And do it well.

Every time.

Make your rivals better.

It's absolutely essential that you be competitive to succeed.

Competitive with yourself, always trying to get better than you are.

Competitive with everyone who does what you do, whether they are in the cubicle next to you or on another continent.

But at the same time, I've always found it hugely beneficial to try to make your rivals better.

For them. And for you.

Early in my career I was surrounded by a group of talented, ambitious young creatives trying to get ahead. We fought for assignments, and we fought for recognition. But we also gave each other tough, honest feedback, and tried to push each other to get better.

If I saw something in someone's work that I could point out to make it smarter, clearer, or cleaner, I would.

They would do the same for me.

Try it.

Not only will your work improve. But your critical thinking and ability to evaluate and guide other people's work will start to be developed.

And those will become invaluable assets as you move into a leadership position or start your own company.

Find your daily happy.

In any business, there'll be good days and bad days.

Most days will have some of each.

And a few days will be truly awful.

Finding a way to interject happiness into at least a portion of each day can go a long way to helping you maintain the positive outlook and equilibrium required to go hard at work every day.

It might be a personal passion project, related or unrelated to work, that you manage to spend a half hour on.

It might be a daily workout, run, or spin class.

It might be a new skill you're learning (juggling?) or a long-time hobby. But whatever it is for you, find it and use it to keep you feeling productive and satisfied on even your worst day.

Be nice.
And not
just to
me.

When I was running my own company, and later, running large global companies, I always made it a practice to talk to people at every level.

A short elevator conversation, a visit to a department I didn't have much contact with, a friendly greeting passing in the hallway goes a long way toward making someone feel a part of things.

But as I later discovered, it had other benefits as well.

That new intern that was so nice to me and senior management?

I was told he was actually a rude demon when dealing with the support staff.

That new Senior VP that seemed so effusive and positive when she met with me and the board?

I was told she was verbally abusive to an assistant who made a small, unintentional and easily correctable mistake.

A good leader will judge the people in the company not just by how that person treats them, but by how they treat everyone else, up and down the corporate ladder.

And while walls may not talk, people do.

Tell the truth to power.

A funny thing happens when you rise to a position of power within any organization. Everyone tells you what they think you want to hear. For a short while, it feels comfortable not to have to fight for your ideas, face criticism and critique, and defend your assumptions.

But for the best leaders, that comfort begins to fade quickly and they begin actively seeking the "truthtellers" that they can count on for an honest, unvarnished opinion.

I was one of those from the earliest days of my career.

Always respectful. But brutally honest.

And coupled with my work, it provided the credibility that allowed me to move quickly up the ranks.

It also solidified my belief that oftentimes, the truthtellers are the people just out of school, whose views are pure, clear and idealistic.

They haven't yet learned to fear, to hide and to hedge.

And hopefully they never will.

The three C's.

You are going to be thrown into many different and unfamiliar situations almost as soon as you begin working.

Presenting your work to superiors that you have never met.

Fielding questions from clients that are unexpected and subjective.

Trying to advance your point of view with resistant co-workers without damaging what will need to be ongoing working relationships.

Three words to remember:

Calm.

Coherent.

Constructive.

Don't be the one in the room getting emotional and losing your cool.

Be the one everyone looks to for calmness and logic.

Don't be the one ranting, interrupting and babbling incessantly.

Be the one listening, then making a clear, coherent case for your rationale.

Don't be the one whining or complaining about a difficult situation.

Be the one who gets past that and is focused on a constructive solution.

Show up, no matter what.

There will be days you will want to stay home and hide.

And there will be meetings you will have a primal fear of attending.

It might be because the work you have to show that day is not anywhere near as good as you wanted it to be.

Or that one of your superiors or clients that you know will be in the room is particularly intimidating.

Go.

One, it is always better to fulfill your commitment, take your beating and be seen as someone who will be there, on good days and bad, than be seen as a coward, a baby, or someone who can't be counted on.

Two, you may hear something during the meeting that will be the basis for a great piece of work you can show the following day.

Three, if you show up with work that is less than your best, you'll have many chances to redeem yourself and it will be quickly forgotten.

If you don't show up, it will never be forgotten.

And four, the overwhelming likelihood is that the meeting will not be nearly as bad as you had feared.

Make it go away.

The leaders in almost every company have tremendous demands on their time and mental capacity.

Client meetings. Management meetings. Board meetings.

Staff meetings. Financial meetings. Planning meetings. Legal meetings. More client meetings.

Plus five crises du jour and a healthy dose of travel.

Which is why nothing is more valuable to us than somebody who can "make it go away."

When I ask you to solve a tricky client issue in London, I don't want you to call my assisstant twice a day asking to come in and give me updates. I don't want you to email me nightly lists of questions asking how to handle each unfolding twist and turn in the process.

If I wanted minute by minute involvement, I would've done it myself.

I want you to come back in a week or a month (or however long is required) later and say, "it's done."

There are only a few people in any company, small or large, who can do that.

And if you are one of them, you're golden.

Think again before SEND

Conflict and confrontation are inherent in business.

And, no doubt, there will be times it will feel like you are being personally attacked.

At these times, you might feel the need to write a nasty-gram or pocket-rocket to make your feelings known and settle the score.

Go ahead and write it.

But don't press SEND.

Because while it will seem to be the perfectly rational and justifiable thing to do, and feel devilishly good as your angry fingers race across the keys, within three minutes you will be searching your keyboard for the "pull it back button." And you will have ceded the moral high-ground and created permanent, forwardable evidence of your immaturity and lack of self-control.

Great does not equal success.

Becoming great at what you do does not guarantee success.

In fact, you will see people all around you who appear to have less talent or skill in their area of expertise than you or others but may be wildly more successful.

You can lament it or chalk it up to life's unfairness, but you'd be doing yourself a disservice.

The simple reality is that some people are intuitively aware of what is required to succeed and have learned to compensate for their shortcomings and build on their strengths in ways that many naturally "talented" people have not had to do.

They become compelling presenters.

They see hidden opportunities that others have overlooked.

They are tenacious.

They make sure that the best of the work they do is seen and associated with them.

Don't begrudge them. Learn from them.

Love,
then
money.

It's no coincidence that the people who are the most successful love what they do.

And they don't love it because they are successful.

They are successful because they love it.

And loved it long before they were successful.

To make the necessary, sustained, year-after-year committment to be truly great at something, you absolutely must find that thing that excites you beyond the pragmatic need to earn a living or a vague dream of "getting rich".

You must also be disciplined enough to walk away from the offers that while seemingly lucrative, will put you on a path away from what you love and are best at.

The short-term increase in your paycheck will look very small just a few years later, and you will have sabotaged your opportunity for the bigger payout, both psychically and monetarily, that you've worked so hard for.

Find what you love.

Stay true to what you love.

If you do, the money will follow.

Have a long and short memory.

Remember things that you did that led to great work.

Forget anyone who tries to convince you that nothing great can be done.

Remember the way it felt to get your first piece produced.

Forget the day-to-day rejection that is a natural by-product of creating.

Remember the people who helped you along the way.

Forget the petty politics that are nothing more than a distraction.

Remember what it felt like to be really tired and keep on pushing.

Forget what time it is when you are working at 2AM.

Remember the first time you stood up for your beliefs and won.

Forget the defeats you suffered when you knew your work was right.

Remember how many "bad" assignments turned into big opportunities.

Forget how many "bad" assignments turned into nothing.

Remember why you got into the business you are in.

Forget how old you are and how long ago that was.

You have two jobs.

Your first job is your job.

Throw yourself into it, and make the most of every opportunity, every day.

But your second job is equally important.

It's the job of managing your career.

Are you in the right company, at the right time, to learn the most, produce the most and advance your career the fastest?

Are you under-challenged and languishing in your position just because it's comfortable and safe?

Should you be doing more to meet the people and build the connections that could push you up to a different level of performance and career advancement?

Are you consciously thinking about your long-term objectives and plan or are you letting time drift by as you just try to survive day-to-day?

Are you actively doing the things you need to do to someday start your own business or are you living in the world of "magical thinking" that assumes it will just "happen"?

Your career is yours, and no one elses.

And it will go by fast.

It's your job to take control of it from day one.

Invest in investing.

You won't be making much right out of school, which is fine. Your mission is to get a job at the best possible place to launch your career, regardless of what they pay you.

And in many cases, the most desirable places pay the least.

But if you dive in, work hard, and begin to produce, that can all change very quickly. In a few short years you can go from just scraping by and paying off your student loans to pulling down some real money.

So, fairly early on, I would recommend you begin learning about money and how to save it, manage it, invest it and grow it.

Read the Wall Street Journal. Find some solid books on investing and study them. Learn about how the stock market, the bond market and the real estate markets work. Your goal should be to gain the knowledge in time to maximize your big earning years, and set yourself on a path to financial independence.

How well you do this will actually play a bigger role in how much wealth you accumulate than what your income is.

The cliché is that "creative people don't need to know anything about dealing with money."

Nothing could be further from the truth.

Start at the end.

We've been conditioned to look at life in neatly prescribed increments.

2 years of middle school.

3 years of high school.

4 years of college.

2 years of graduate school (maybe).

But what about the next 30 after that?

There is no Google Map for your career, or your life.

You'll have to make your own.

One way is to start at the end of your career and life and ask yourself
what you will feel good having accomplished.

To be recognized by your peers as one of the best at what you do?

To change the business you're in for the better?

To invent something that will make people's lives better?

To start your own business?

To make lots of money and support the causes you believe in?

To have and raise a happy family?

There are no right or wrong answers.

But by defining what is ultimately important to you, the day-to-day,
year-to-year decisions will become easier to make.

about

A leader in advertising for over twenty-five years, Gary Goldsmith has created memorable campaigns for many of the world's most respected brands, including IBM, Mercedes Benz, Heineken, Sony, UPS, Coca Cola, Volkswagen, Everlast and ESPN.

Gary has won awards from every major international advertising competition, including The Cannes Film Festival, where he also twice represented the United States as a judge. He was featured in the Wall Street Journal Creative Leaders Series, and his work is included in the permanent collection of The Museum of Modern Art.

Formerly chairman and chief creative officer of his own internationally recognized agency, Goldsmith/Jeffrey, Gary also served as chairman and chief creative officer of Lowe North America and creative director of TBWA\Chiat\Day NY. Prior to beginning his career at the legendary agency Doyle Dane Bernbach, he earned a B.A. from the University of Texas at Austin and a B.F.A. from Art Center College of Design.

Gary is currently a founding partner of Underhead.com, a virtual, global creative network, and the chair of advertising at Art Center College of Design in Pasadena.

Thank you.

To Stan Richards, Roy Grace, Helmut Krone, Bob Gage, Joe Toto, Bob Kuperman, John Miyauchi, Mel Sant, Sir Frank Lowe, Phyllis Robinson and my father, Charles Goldsmith for being important mentors for me. Whether they knew it or not.

94540815R00029

Made in the USA
Lexington, KY
31 July 2018